Rainbow the Cat Goes to the Farm
彩虹猫：出发去农场

Author: Anna Banas-Chen
作者：安娜·贝纳斯陈恒月
Illustrator: Julia Wu/Lillian Lin
插画：吴林林/林雪莹
Translator: Jessica Wu
译者：吴宜

This book teaches kids about farm animals.
Come along with Rainbow the Cat to learn fun
facts about animals found on the farm.

这本书将给孩子们介绍有关农场动物的知
识。跟彩虹猫一起学习有关农场动物的有
趣知识吧！

This book has been translated into Chinese, French and Spanish.
此书已被译成中文、法语及西班牙文。

Acknowledgments

This book is dedicated to my grandparents Bob and Agnes, Mingshou, and my parents Mike and Emma. Thank you for your love and support for my second book! Nai Nai Yimei Ye (Judy), I miss you.

Special thanks to my teacher Mrs. Janice Currie for teaching me everything, and my horseback riding instructor Heather Reynolds for teaching me about horses.

谨以此书献给我的爷爷鲍伯、奶奶艾格纳斯、外公陈明寿、爸爸麦克、妈妈秋慧。谢谢您们的爱和支持我的第二本书的出版！外婆叶依妹，我思念您。

衷心感谢珍妮斯.科瑞老师的谆谆教诲还有我的骑马教练希瑟对我的教导。

One day after school, Rainbow the Cat went with her mom to the farm. She was excited. She wanted to learn how to ride horses. Rainbow the Cat did not realize how many other animals can be found on the farm. Do you know what animals you can see at a farm?

一天，彩虹猫放学后和妈妈一起去了农场。她很兴奋。她跟妈妈说自己想学骑马。彩虹猫没有意识到农场里除了马还有很多其他动物。你知道在农场里能看到什么动物吗？

welcome
Best Farm
WOOD   WATER
CERTIFIED FAMILY FOREST
RECREATION   WILDLIFE
WOOD   WATER
CERTIFIED TREE FARM
RECREATION   WILDLIFE

When she got there, she saw some sheep eating grass,
some chickens chasing each other and ducks in the pond.

当她来到了农场，她看到一群绵羊在吃草，
几只鸡在互相追逐，一群鸭子在池塘里戏水。

Rainbow met Heather, her horseback riding instructor.

彩虹猫第一次见到了她的骑马教练希瑟。

Heather showed Rainbow the Cat her horse named Lemon. Rainbow took her first lesson in horseback riding. Soon, her lesson was over, but she still had to brush Lemon and feed her dinner. Rainbow put the food in her stall, and the water in Lemon's bucket.

希瑟把那匹叫柠檬的马介绍给了彩虹猫。彩虹猫开始了她的第一节骑马课。这节课很快就结束了，但课后她还得给柠檬刷毛，喂晚饭。彩虹猫把食物放在柠檬的食槽里，把水放在它的桶里。

<u>Fun facts about horses:</u>
- Baby horses are called foals. Foals can run shortly after being born.
- Horses can sleep lying down and standing up.
- Horses can run up to 45 miles per hour.
- Horses are large, strong and smart.

<u>关于马的有趣小知识:</u>
- 幼马被称为马驹。马出生后不久就能跑了。
- 马既可以躺着睡觉,也可以站着睡觉。
- 马每小时能跑45英里。
- 马很高大、强壮,也很聪明。

<u>What do horses eat and how do people feed them?</u>
Horses eat hay, grass and grains at mealtime. You can give them fruits and vegetables as snacks. Horses need a lot of water to drink.

<u>马吃什么?人们都如何喂马?</u>
马将干草、草和谷物当做主食。你可以给他们水果和蔬菜当零食。马需要喝很多水。

Next, Rainbow the Cat was going to see the chickens. They had white and brown feathers. Angelo was the name of the rooster.

接下来, 彩虹猫要去看鸡。它们有着白色和棕色的羽毛。那只
公鸡的名字叫安吉洛。

<u>Fun facts about chickens and roosters:</u>
- A young chicken is called a chick.
- Chickens live in a chicken coop.
- An adult male chicken is called a "rooster". An adult female is called a "hen".
- Hens lay eggs which hatch into chicks.
- Roosters can crow.

<u>关于鸡和公鸡的有趣小知识:</u>
- 鸡小的时候叫做鸡雏。
- 鸡住在鸡笼里。
- 成年雄性鸡被称为"公鸡"; 成年雌性鸡被称为"母鸡"。
- 母鸡下蛋后会孵出小鸡。
- 公鸡会打鸣。

<u>What do chickens eat and how do people feed them?</u>
Chickens like to scratch and peck at the ground for bugs. Chickens also eat grains, and vegetables. Chickens drink water from a water dish in their chicken coop. Do not use your hand to feed them because they can bite you.

<u>鸡吃什么?人们都如何喂鸡?</u>
鸡喜欢在地上啄虫子。当然, 它们也喜欢谷物和蔬菜。它们会在鸡笼
里从水盆中喝水。
但是请注意!不要用你的手去喂它们, 因为它们会啄你的手。

Rainbow the Cat walked over to see the sheep. They were fuzzy and cute! Rainbow saw a baby sheep. His name was Oscar, he loved to frolic and jump!

之后，彩虹猫走去看了看羊。它们毛茸茸的，真可爱！彩虹猫看见了一只名叫奥斯卡的小绵羊，它喜欢嬉闹和跳跃！

<u>Fun facts about sheep:</u>
- Young sheep are called lambs.
- Female sheep are called ewes. Adult male sheep are known as rams.
- Sheep live in a large group called a flock.
- Sheep have a thick coat called wool, it can be used to make clothing and blankets.

<u>关于绵羊的小知识：</u>
- 小绵羊叫做羔羊。
- 雌性的羊叫做母羊。
- 成年雄性绵羊被称为公羊。
- 羊喜欢群居生活，一群羊称为羊群。
- 绵羊身上有一层厚的皮毛，叫做羊毛，它可以用来做衣服和毯子。

<u>What do sheep eat and how do people feed them?</u>
Sheep eat grass from pastures. When you feed sheep, you put your hands flat, and hold the food on your palm, and they will use their tongue to eat it.

<u>绵羊吃什么？人们都如何喂绵羊？</u>
绵羊吃牧场上的草。当你喂羊的时候，把手放平，让食物平摊在手掌上，它们会用舌头舔着来把食物吃掉。

Rainbow looked in the next pasture, there was a bull named Bob.

彩虹猫看了看旁边的牧场，那里有一头叫鲍勃的公牛。

<u>Fun facts about cows:</u>
- Baby cows are called calves.
- Cows cannot see the colors red and green.
- Cows have good hearing.
- Everyday a cow can spend 8 hours eating, 8 hours chewing
and 8 hours sleeping.

<u>关于奶牛的有趣小知识:</u>
- 年幼的牛被称为小牛。
- 牛的视觉分辨不出红色和绿色。
- 牛有很好的听觉。
- 牛每天可以花8小时吃饭，8小时咀嚼，8小时睡觉。

<u>What do cows eat and how do people feed them?</u>
Baby calves drink milk. Cows eat grains mixed with hay, corn silage (entire corn plant chopped and fermented). People put the food in the cow barn or put the food in the feeding bucket. Cows also love to eat grass.

<u>牛吃什么?人们都如何喂牛?</u>
小牛喝牛奶。牛吃混合干草的谷物，玉米青贮饲料(就是把整株玉米切碎并让它发酵)。人们把食物放在牛棚里或者放在喂食桶里。另外，牛也喜欢吃草。

Rainbow went to check out the pig pen. Emma the pig rolled around in the mud.

彩虹猫去猪圈看了看。小猪艾玛正在泥里打滚。

<u>Fun facts about pigs:</u>
- Pigs are intelligent animals.
- Pigs are omnivores, meaning they eat both plants and other animals.
- Pigs have an excellent sense of smell.
- Some people like to keep pigs as pets.
- Wild pigs are called boar.

<u>关于猪的有趣小知识:</u>
- 猪其实很聪明。
- 猪是杂食动物，也就是说它们既吃植物也吃肉。
- 猪有极佳的嗅觉。
- 有些人喜欢把猪当作宠物养。
- 在野生环境里生活的猪被称为野猪。

<u>What do pigs eat and how do people feed them?</u>
Pigs eat grains, fruits and vegetables. Do not feed pigs with your hand, they can bite!

<u>猪吃什么?人们都怎么喂猪?</u>
猪吃谷物、水果和蔬菜。注意，不要用手
去喂猪，它们会咬人!

Rainbow explored a wooden hutch. That is where the bunny Agnes lived.

接着，彩虹猫去了一个木制的小木屋。那就是兔子艾格尼丝住的地方。

<u>Fun facts about bunnies:</u>
- Bunnies are born with their eyes closed and without fur.
- A young rabbit is called a kit.
- A female rabbit is called a doe.
- A male rabbit is called a buck.
- Rabbits are herbivores, they only eat plants.
- Rabbit's teeth never stop growing!
- A rabbit can make a great pet.

<u>关于兔子的有趣小知识：</u>
- 兔子刚出生时眼睛是闭着的，而且身上没有毛。
- 小兔子被称为幼兔。
- 母兔子被称为雌兔。
- 公兔子被称为雄兔。
- 兔子是食草动物，它们只吃植物。
- 兔子的牙齿永远都在长！
- 兔子可以成为很好的宠物。

<u>What do rabbits eat and how do people feed them?</u>
Plants and vegetables. Especially carrots! People can put the food
on the ground, or in a bowl and they will eat it.

<u>兔子吃什么？人们都如何喂兔子？</u>
它们吃植物和蔬菜，尤其喜欢胡萝卜！人们可以把食物放在地上，
或者放在碗里让它们吃。

Agnes
WAGON

Rainbow saw a goose named Mike, running around.
彩虹猫看见一只叫麦克的鹅在到处跑。

<u>Fun facts about geese:</u>
- Geese migrate every year.
- Geese can live almost anywhere.
- Geese fly in a "V" shape.
- Geese are related to Ducks and Swans.
- DO NOT play with geese, they can chase and bite you!

<u>关于鹅的有趣小知识:</u>
- 有些鹅每年迁徙。
- 鹅几乎可以在任何地方生活。
- 鹅飞的时候成V字形。
- 鹅是鸭子和天鹅的亲戚。
- 不要和鹅玩耍，它们会追着人跑，还会咬人！

<u>What do geese eat and how do people feed them?</u>
Geese eat seeds, nuts, grass, plants and berries. People can feed them by spreading food out in the grass, or in a large bowl.

<u>鹅吃什么？人们都如何喂鹅？</u>
鹅吃种子、坚果、草、植物和浆果。人们可以把食物撒在草地上，或者放在一个大碗里喂它们。

Nearby, Kiki the kitten napped in the sun.

在彩虹猫的身旁，小猫琪琪在阳光下打盹。

<u>Fun facts about kittens:</u>
- Kittens are blind and deaf until 2 to 3 weeks old.
They need their mom during this time.
- All kittens are born with blue eyes.
- Kittens have a strong sense of smell.
- Kittens have 26 teeth.

<u>关于小猫的有趣小知识:</u>
- 小猫在2到3周大之前都看不见和听不见的。
这段时间它们都需要母猫的照顾。
- 所有的小猫出生时眼睛都是蓝色的。
- 小猫的嗅觉很灵敏。
- 小猫有26颗牙齿。

<u>What do kittens eat and how do people feed them?</u>
- Kittens can't drink cow milk. It will upset their stomach.
They can drink special kitten formula if needed.
- Kittens can eat wet or dry kitten food, or
home-made food out of a bowl.
- Kittens love fish.

<u>小猫吃什么?人们都如何喂小猫?</u>
- 小猫不能喝牛奶，这会让它们的胃不舒服。如果需要的话，
它们可以喝特殊的小猫配方奶。
- 小猫可以吃湿的或干的猫粮，或用碗装着煮熟的食物给它们吃。
- 小猫爱吃鱼肉。

27

Next, Rainbow saw a big bird, it was a turkey. Her name was Amy.

接着，彩虹猫看见了一只大鸟，它是一只漂亮的火鸡。它的名字叫艾米。

<u>Fun facts about turkeys:</u>
- A group of turkeys is called a flock.
- Turkeys have 2 stomachs.
- Male turkeys have loose skin by their beak called a waddle.

关于火鸡的有趣小知识：
- 一群火鸡被称为火鸡群。
- 每只火鸡有两个胃。
- 雄性火鸡的喙部有松散的皮，叫做红色肉瓣。

<u>What do turkeys eat and how do people feed them?</u>
Turkeys are herbivores. They like to eat the growing tips of the grass.
They also enjoy lettuce, tomatoes, sweet corn and summer squash.

火鸡吃什么？人们都如何喂火鸡？
火鸡是食草动物。它们喜欢吃正在生长的嫩嫩的草尖。
它们还喜欢吃生菜、西红柿、甜玉米和西葫芦。

Rainbow heard a sound coming from the barn. "Hee-haw!"
What animal makes that sound? It was Leo, a donkey foal.

彩虹猫听到谷仓里有声音。"嘿呵!"什么动物会发出这种声音?
原来是利奥,一头小驴。

<u>Fun facts about donkeys:</u>
- Donkeys are related to horses and zebras.
- A boy donkey is called a jack.
- A girl donkey is called a jenny.
- Donkeys can be stubborn.

<u>关于驴的有趣小知识:</u>
- 驴与马和斑马是亲戚。
- 小公驴叫杰克。
- 小母驴叫珍妮。
- 驴可能会很固执。

<u>What do donkeys eat and how do people feed them?</u>
Donkeys eat hay and grass from the pasture.
You can feed them hay and grains in the barn, too.

<u>驴吃什么?人们都如何喂驴?</u>
驴吃牧场上的牧草和青草。你也可以在谷仓里给它
们喂干草和谷物。

Quack! Quack! Rainbow saw Ben the duck swimming in the pond with his friends.

"嘎!嘎!"彩虹猫看见了本,那是一只鸭子。它和它的朋友们在池塘里游泳。

<u>Fun facts about ducks:</u>
- A baby duck is called a duckling.
- Ducks are water birds, like geese and swans.
- Ducks' feathers are waterproof.
- Very few ducks actually "quack", however, they can make a lot of other sounds.

<u>关于鸭子的有趣小知识:</u>
- 出生不久的鸭子叫做小鸭子。
- 鸭子是水中的鸟,像鹅和天鹅一样。
- 鸭子的羽毛是防水的。
- 很少鸭子真的会嘎嘎叫,但是它们可以发出很多其他的声音。

<u>What do ducks eat and how do people feed them?</u>
Ducks eat grass, aquatic plants, insects, seeds, fruit, fish, vegetables and grains.
You can throw the food to them in the pond or on the grass.

<u>鸭子吃什么?人们都怎么喂鸭子?</u>
鸭子吃草、水生植物、昆虫、种子、水果、鱼、蔬菜和谷物。
你可以把食物扔到池塘里或草地上喂它们。

In the pasture, there was a baby goat named Lydia.
Rainbow stood on the fence to say hello.

在牧场上，有一只小山羊叫莉迪亚。彩虹猫站在篱笆上向它打招呼。

<u>Fun facts about goats:</u>
- Young goats are called kids.
- Goat kids learn to stand right after they are born.
- Kids begin climbing and jumping when they are a week old.
- Goat kids like to snuggle, just like human kids.
- Goat kids make sounds that are called a bleat. Mother and kid goats recognize each other's bleats.

<u>关于山羊的有趣小知识:</u>
- 年幼山羊被称为小山羊。
- 山羊宝宝一出生就会站立。
- 小山羊在一周大的时候就开始爬和跳了。
- 小山羊喜欢拥抱，就像人类的小孩一样，喜欢被拥抱。
- 山羊的叫声被称为咩声。母山羊和小山羊可以识别彼此的叫声。

<u>What do goats eat and how do people feed them?</u>
Goats are known for eating everything! Even cardboard, tin cans and clothing.(But that isn't healthy for them!)- Goats like to eat plants, leaves, bushes, grass and hay. If you want to feed them grains, you can hold your hand flat, they will lick it off your hand.

<u>山羊吃什么?人们都怎么喂山羊?</u>
- 山羊是出了名的什么都吃!它们甚至吃纸板、锡罐和衣服，
但这对它们来说都非常不健康!
- 山羊喜欢吃植物，比如树叶、灌木、青草和干草。如果你想给它们喂食物，你可以把食物放手中，然后把手放平，它们就会舔走你手上的食物。

35

Rainbow heard some noise nearby; puppies were wrestling in the grass!
Rainbow watched Sancho the puppy play.

彩虹猫听到附近有动静,原来是小狗在草地上摔跤!彩虹猫看着小狗
山初在玩耍。

<u>Fun facts about puppies:</u>
- Puppies spend 15 to 20 hours a day sleeping.
- Puppies become 'adults' when they turn one year old.
- Puppies are born without teeth.
- Newborn puppies can't poop.
- Puppies can be twins. Double the cuteness.

<u>关于小狗的有趣小知识:</u>
- 小狗每天要睡15到20个小时。
- 幼犬在一岁时就会变成"成年犬"。
- 幼犬出生时没有牙齿。
- 新生的小狗不会便便。
- 有些小狗生出来是双胞胎。那就是双倍的可爱!

<u>What do puppies eat and how do people feed them?</u>
- Puppies drink their mother's milk till 4 weeks old,
and then they start eating dog food.
- You can put the food in their bowl.
- They drink water or special puppies' formula milk.

<u>小狗吃什么?人们都怎么喂狗?</u>
幼犬出生后的头四周内会喝母狗的奶,然后它们就开始吃狗粮。你可
以把食物放在它们的碗里。它们可以喝水或特殊的幼犬配方奶。

SANCHO

Zac, a llama came by to see Rainbow.

扎克是一只大羊驼，它朝着彩虹猫走过来。

<u>Fun facts about llamas:</u>
- Llamas are related to camels.
- Llamas help people carry heavy loads.
- People use their wool to make fabric for clothing.

<u>关于大羊驼的有趣小知识:</u>
- 大羊驼与骆驼是近亲。
- 大羊驼能帮助人们搬运货物。
- 人们用它们的毛做衣服的布料。

<u>What do llamas eat and how do people feed them?</u>
Llamas are herbivores, they only eat plants. Hold your hand flat and they will eat the food from your hand.

<u>大羊驼吃什么? 人们都如何喂大羊驼?</u>
大羊驼是食草动物，它们只吃植物。你可以把食物放手中，然后把手放平，他们就会吃掉你手里的食物。

There was a pony on the farm. Her name was Astrid. Rainbow meowed hello to Astrid.

农场里有一匹小马。它叫阿斯特丽德。彩虹猫向阿斯特丽德问好。

<u>Fun facts about ponies:</u>
- Ponies are small horses.
- Young ponies are called foals.
- Shetland ponies are small but strong.
- Well-trained ponies are good for children to learn to ride.

<u>关于小马的有趣小知识:</u>
- 小马是小型种的马。
- 年幼的马称为马驹。
- 设得兰矮种马虽小但很强壮。训练有素的小马很适合初学骑马的小朋友。

<u>What do ponies eat and how to feed them?</u>
- Ponies mostly eat hay and grass.
- Sometimes they eat grains such as, corn or oats.
- You can put their food in their bucket.

<u>小马吃什么?人们都如何喂小马?</u>
- 小马主要吃干草和草。
- 有时它们会吃谷物,如玉米或燕麦。
- 你可以把它们的食物放在它们的桶里。

"Hiss!" Rainbow the cat heard something in the pasture where the sheep were eating. It was a "rainbow" snake! Rainbow was afraid until she remembered her mom said not to be afraid of snakes. Rainbow was thinking, for this rainbow snake, Anna was a good name. Snakes are not farm animals, but you can find snakes in pastures and in nearby woods.

彩虹猫在羊牧场上听到有轻微的"嘶"的声音。哦，她看到一条"彩虹色"的蛇！彩虹猫很害怕，可是她也想起妈妈跟她说过，看到蛇不要害怕。彩虹猫心想，不如为这条彩虹蛇起安娜这个名字吧。蛇通常不是住在农场里的动物，但你可能在牧场里或附近的树林里找到它们。

Fun facts about snakes:
- Snakes can swallow their food, called prey, whole.
- Snakes shed their skin as they grow bigger.
- Snakes can be venomous or non-venomous, it is best to leave them alone.
- Snakes are carnivores, or meat eaters, just like Rainbow the Cat.
- Snakes are not slimy! Their scales are smooth and help them slither.

关于蛇的有趣小知识:
- 蛇可以直接完整地吞下它们的猎物。
- 蛇变大后会蜕皮。
- 有些蛇是有毒的，有些却是无毒的，但最好还是不要碰它们。
- 蛇是肉食动物，就像彩虹猫一样。
- 蛇不是黏糊糊的！它们的鳞片很光滑，可以帮助它们滑行。

Now it was time to leave, Rainbow the Cat had a great time. She loves the farm and she cannot wait to come back to visit again.

现在要回家了。彩虹猫玩得非常开心。她十分喜欢这个农场，她兴奋地期待着再次回来。

See you!
Thanks for
comeing

吴林林(Julia)，贡献了此书的插画的灵感和创意。她是8岁深圳的三年级小学生，富有天赋，爱好美术和手工，自小周游列国，了解各国文化艺术，对小动物有浓厚兴趣，希望以后有更多机会了解动物与世界并立志在世界著名的艺术学院学习。

Lilin·Julia·Wu is the little painter of this book. She is an 8 year old third grader living in Shenzhen, China. Julia is very talented and she loves arts and making handcrafts. Since she was younger, she has traveled around the world and become familiar with different cultures and arts. She is an animal lover. Julia is looking forward to have more opportunities to discover animals and the world. She has the ambition to be educated in the greatest arts university.

林雪莹（Lillian）此书的插画师，毕业于伦敦艺术大学。
Xueying Lin, the co-illustrator of this book graduated from University of the Arts London.

吴宜(Jesscia)，出生于2003年，青少年创业家，青爱基金校园形象大使，Sparkling 青少年创业平台创始人。
曾受邀参加达沃斯世界经济论坛、WIN全球女性领袖论坛等。
热爱创作、科技创新与创业，具有强烈的社会责任感参与了许多支教项目以及与儿童、青少年教育相关的公益组织项目。
Yi·Jessica·Wu, born in 2003, is a young entrepreneur, campus image ambassador of Qing-Ai foundation, and founder of Sparkling Youth.

She has been invited to participate in Davos world economic forum, WIN global women leaders forum, etc.

She loves creation, scientific and technological innovation and entrepreneurship, has a strong sense of social responsibility. She also has participated in many supporting education projects and public welfare organization projects related to children's and youth's education.

The profit from this book will be donated to:
这本书的收益将全部捐献给以下公益机构:

(1)   United Nations The Food and Agriculture Organization (FAO)

联合国粮食及农业组织(FAO)是联合国的专门机构,领导国际社会努力战胜饥饿。粮农组织的目标是实现所有人的粮食安全,并确保人们定期获得足够的优质食物,以过上积极健康的生活。粮农组织有194个成员国,在全球130多个国家/地区开展工作。我们认为,每个人都可以在消除饥饿方面发挥作用。加入我们,创建"零饥饿"世界。

(2)   The Zoo in Forest Park & Education Center

森林动物园和教育中心位于美国马萨诸塞州春田市,是拥有127年历史的公益组织。它致力于野生动植物的教育、保护和康复工作。森林动物园里有超过225种外来和本地物种,其中大多数是因为受伤、疾病、永久性残疾或其他因素而需要被康复的动物们。

(3)   Pony Club

美国小马俱乐部公司(Pony Clubs, Inc.)于1954年成立的公益机构,负责教授骑马和马术训练。它是1929年成立的英国小马俱乐部及其马术学院的分支机构。现在,小马俱乐部已扩展到世界许多国家,其主要目标是通过马术促进体育精神,管理才能和领导能力。

Book reviews: / 书评：

"安娜·贝纳斯陈，一位杰出的小朋友又写出了一本杰出的书。彩虹猫又回来了，这次它去农场探索，并介绍农场里的小动物们。这本书也适合不同年龄段的人。彩虹猫不仅与动物们在农场相遇，而且分享了有关动物们的有趣的小知识。公鸡安吉洛(Angelo)首次登场亮相，当猫彩虹去拜访这些动物时，它们是那么的活灵活现。我等不及要看彩虹猫和安娜接下来又会要带我们去什么地方。"
-安吉洛·普普洛，国会众议员、出口发展委员会主席

"安娜·贝纳斯陈的《彩虹猫：去农场》是又一出迷人的单曲。我最喜欢此书的有关每种动物的"有趣的小知识"的部分。例如，我了解到猪具有极好的嗅觉。尽管我的童年已经逝去许久了，但安娜的文本和朱莉娅·吴有趣的插图的完美结合立刻引起了我的兴趣。这是安娜此书的魅力所在 - 她的故事能让不同年龄的人，从多元文化的层面上引起共鸣。在充满挑战和压力的今天，安娜对世界的新认识，让读者觉得振奋并学习到了新知识。我热切盼望彩虹猫系列中的下一本书，我也很高兴与我所有认识的人分享安娜的作品。"
–克里斯蒂娜·哈雷特，博士，国际畅销书作者，知名临床心理学家，副教授，TEDx演讲者

"安娜又出书了！第二本书，彩虹猫到农场探索，深入到农场的一个又一个有趣的角落。彩虹猫的整个农场之旅带着读者认识了许多不同的动物-从鹅到猪，再到兔子，再到牛，还有很多其他的动物！读者将体验彩虹猫的新冒险之旅，每一页书都能提高小朋友的阅读能力，并学习了解有关动物的知识。这本书真棒，在故事中学习，实在令人难以置信！"
–朱莉娅·古丁，哈佛教育学院，国际教育工作者

"哇，这对彩虹猫来说，是一次了不起的旅行。与孩子们一起阅读此书，了解这些农场动物的生活，肯定会让我们嘴角上扬微笑，感到和平与爱。在这样的艰难时期中，和平与爱就是我们每个家庭、父母与孩子所向往的，这个美好的世界所需要的。我期待着彩虹猫的下一次旅程，我相信那将是另一种充满想象力的经历。"
–林海安，博士，美国联邦注册律师，兼职教授

"安娜在她的第二本书中，带领读者在农场里进行了一次冒险之旅。我喜欢阅读彩虹猫在农场里遇到的各种各样的朋友，以及关于每种动物的有趣的小知识！安娜的好奇心和她对动物的热情在她的作品中很明显地体现了出来。这就是彩虹猫在故事中探索以及学习知识的综合点，非常令人兴奋。我期待看到安娜接下来将彩虹猫带到哪里！"
–梁蕊馨，马萨诸塞州杰出少女